C000142087

Our Ladies of Perpetual Succour

Alan Warner is the author of eight novels: *Morvern Callar* (which was made into a film starring Samantha Morton), *These Demented Lands*, *The Sopranos*, *The Man Who Walks*, *The Worms Can Carry Me to Heaven*, *The Stars in the Bright Sky* (which was longlisted for the 2010 Man Booker Prize) and *The Deadman's Pedal*, which won the 2013 James Tait Black Prize. His most recent novel, *Their Lips Talk of Mischief*, was published by Faber & Faber.

Lee Hall was born in Newcastle in 1966. He started writing for radio in 1995, winning awards for *I Luv You Jimmy Spud*, *Spoonface Steinberg* and *Blood Sugar*, all of which made the journey to other media. His screenplay for *Billy Elliot* was nominated for an Oscar and was adapted into a multi-award-winning stage musical. *The Pitmen Painters* received the Evening Standard Best Play Award and TMA Best New Play Award. He has worked as writer-in-residence for Live Theatre, Newcastle, and the Royal Shakespeare Company, and has adapted many plays for the stage, including Goldoni's *A Servant to Two Masters* (Young Vic/RSC), Brecht's *Mr Puntila and His Man Matti* (Right Size/ Almeida) and Heijermans' *The Good Hope* (National Theatre).

LEE HALL

Our Ladies of Perpetual Succour

adapted from the novel *The Sopranos* by

ALAN WARNER

FABER & FABER

First published in 2015
by Faber and Faber Limited
74–77 Great Russell Street
London WC1B 3DA

Reptinted 2017

Typeset by Country Setting, Kingsdown, Kent CT14 8ES
Printed in England by CPI Group (UK) Ltd, Croydon CR0 4YY

A CIP record for this book is available from the British Library

ISBN 978-0-571-34031-6

2 4 6 8 10 9 7 5 3 1

Introduction

I read Alan Warner's *The Sopranos* when it was first
published. I laughed out loud more at this book than at
any other I can remember. I immediately recognised these
girls. They were on the one hand incredibly modern but
on the other they were part of a very old vein of British
literature going right back to the Wife of Bath and beyond.
Here was life in all its vitality. The sacred and the
profane smashed together. It was at once breathtakingly
rude and transgressive but also exquisitely wrought with
melancholy. The girls in the book seemed to get a
heartbreaking vantage on the limitations of their lives
by the act of exceeding them. It seemed so right about
the rites of passage of adolescence. The formal rites are
not sufficient so we invent our own. We dice with death
to prove we are alive. We act with total irresponsibility
to prove we are grown-up. We do it in groups to feel
uniquely individual. The book is fraught with these
contradictions, but they are contradictions which we
know not to be contradictory at all. That is how life is.

So *The Sopranos* seemed perfect for the stage. Of course
Vicky Featherstone at that time was Artistic Director at
the National Theatre of Scotland and had long wanted
to do it – but it was a chance meeting between us where
I expressed my immense admiration for the book which
led to us actually doing it on stage. After several years of
negotiating over rights, Alan Warner gave us permission
to give it a go – and here it is. It seemed to us that the
girls of *Our Ladies* should tell their own story and when
we realised that they should play all the parts, the style
of the production fell into shape.

In many ways this play is more like a gig than a play. It is set, I suppose, in the rather unprepossessing Mantrap – the only nightclub in the girls' home town. But that's alright because the play is about how the everyday is translated into the sacred, how the most sordid circumstances of our lives are the conditions of our deliverance, because they are ours. The play is about very ordinary acts of resistance and how that resistance transfigures us and affords us transcendence from the mire of our lives. These are acts of glory, manifest with the full force of life. May we all take benediction from *Our Ladies of Perpetual Succour*.

Characters

Orla

Chell

Kay

Manda

Kylah

Fionnula

Our Ladies of Perpetual Succour was first performed by the National Theatre of Scotland and Live Theatre at the Traverse Theatre, Edinburgh, on 19 August 2015. The cast, in alphabetical order, was as follows:

Orla Melissa Allan
Chell Caroline Deyga
Kay Karen Fishwick
Manda Kirsty MacLaren
Kylah Frances Mayli McCann
Fionnula Dawn Sievewright

The Band
Amy Shackcloth (*band leader/keyboards*)
Becky Brass (*percussion*)
Emily Linden (*guitar*)

Director Vicky Featherstone
Designer Chloe Lamford
Lighting Designer Lizzie Powell
Sound Designer Mike Walker
Music Arranger and Supervisor Martin Lowe
Choreographer Imogen Knight

Our Ladies of Perpetual Succour in the National Theatre of Scotland and Live Theatre production was first presented in the West End at the Duke of York's Theatre, London, on 9 May 2017 by Sonia Friedman Productions, Scott M. Delman, Gail Berman Theatricals and Tulchin Bartner Productions, in association with Rupert Gavin, William Court Cohen, Ashley M. DeSimone and Jeremiah J. Harris. The West End cast was as follows:

Chell Caroline Deyga
Kay Karen Fishwick
Orla Isis Hainsworth
Manda Kirsty MacLaren
Kylah Frances Mayli McCann
Fionnula Dawn Sievewright

The Band
Amy Shackcloth (*Musical Director / keyboard*)
Lilly Howard (*Assistant Musical Director / keyboard*)
Becky Brass (*percussion*)
Emily Linden (*guitar*)

Director Vicky Featherstone
Music sourced, arranged and supervised by Martin Lowe
Designer Chloe Lamford
Choreographer Imogen Knight
Lighting Designer Lizzie Powell
Sound Designer Mike Walker
Casting Directors Amy Ball CDG and Laura Donnelly CDG

Author's Note

My adaptation of Alan Warner's novel *The Sopranos* is
written for six actors who play all the roles. The conceit
of our production was that the girls in the story have
made a show which they are putting on in the Mantrap –
the grotty nightclub which features in the story. The
production was built around the idea of them using
their choral repertoire but also a whole bunch of cover
versions, mostly of Electric Light Orchestra numbers.
So the style of the show is more like a gig than a piece
of ordinary theatre, and certainly the production was
'punk' in its spirit, paying no heed to conventions of
realism and using whatever was on hand to suggest
action and place.

OUR LADIES OF PERPETUAL SUCCOUR

The girls start singing 'Lift thine eyes' from Mendelssohn's oratorio Elijah.

> Lift thine eyes, O lift thine eyes,
> To the mountains, whence cometh
> Whence cometh help.
>
> Thy help cometh from the Lord
> The maker of heaven and earth,
> He hath said, thy foot shall not be moved.
>
> Thy keeper shall never slumber
> Shall never slumber never slumber.
>
> Lift thine eyes O lift thine eyes
> To the mountains whence cometh
> Whence cometh whence cometh help.

Chell This is fucking ridiculous.

Manda Six in the fucking morning and Condom's not even here.

Fionnula Even if we win this fucking competition they'll have us in a shitey hotel overnight like girls from last year.

Kylah *Fionnula the cooler –*

Orla *– lives in a council house, bought with the money from her granda.*

Manda The hotel didn't even have bathrooms.

Chell *Manda Tassy.*

Kylah *Mam fucked off.*

Chell *Lives with her da.*

Fionnula *Never shuts up about –*

Manda *– ma sister!*

Chell Don't panic – if we stick together there's no ways we'll even get to the second round . . .

Manda *Chell MacDougal –*

Kylah *– lives up the Complex.*

Chell *I've had a lot of tragedy in ma family.* We'll be back on the fucking bus in time for some slow jigs and a quick sailor's hornpipe in the Mantrap.

They cheer.

Orla Aye, but we'll never get past that new bouncer.

Fionnula *Orla McAlister –*

Chell *– from the villages.*

Manda *Diagnosed with cancer –*

Kylah *– but recently returned from Lourdes.*

Manda I know, one of us could fuck him.

Kylah Manda, he's from the island!

Fionnula *Kylah McManus.*

Manda *Parents own their own house.*

Chell *Sings in a band.*

Fionnula Cunt's only on the door cos he couldnae get a chef's job.

Chell Aye, he can only tell the ages of sheep.

Manda From behind.

Kay Morning, everybody!

Kylah *Kay Clarke.*

Fionnula *Stuck up, sugar-wouldn't-melt-in-her-mouth, off-to-university, goody-fucking-two-shoes.*

Manda Oh, my God! Submarine!

Kylah There it is, I can see the conning tower!

Chell It'll be heaving in the Mantrap the night.

Fionnula Fucking typical – the one night we're in the capital.

Manda Ma sister says that when submariner-ers, right, get a cut or something, cos they've been away under water for so long, it doesn't stop bleeding!

Fionnulla And apparently when they spunk their wank – it just keeps coming and coming. Till the whole fucking submarines drowning in jizz down there.

Chell Here lie one hundred brave sailors drowned in their own jizz.

Kylah Let's just make sure we get back before the slow dances – we'll be getting hurls around the bay.

Manda Aye but just remember Shuna MacLaughlin.

Kylah Shuna MacLaughlin didnae get pregnant off a submariner. It was one of those Pakistani lads off the van.

Orla Look, here she is the noo.

Shuna!

Kay Clarke puts a pillow up her jumper and becomes Shuna MacLaughlin.

Shuna MacLaughlin (*Kay*) Hello there, girls.

All Hi, Shuna.

They all gather round.

15

Shuna (*Kay*) Yous all off to the Finals then?

Orla Aye. Where you going?

Shuna (*Kay*) I'm up to the pre-natal at the Chest.

Manda At this time in the morn?

Shuna (*Kay*) Oh aye, it's so ya get used to the idea of sleepless nights when the baby comes.

Manda The cunts, eh?

Shuna (*Kay*) Ah tell you, yous think pre-natal's bad yous should see the fucking post-natal, ah swear on the Bible, three lassies from the villages come in a horse box pulled by their boyfriend's tractor, three of them, there in the shite wi' their little wee babies and all.

Chell That'll be Dempster the Dumpster.

Shuna (*Kay*) They've got signs in the caff above the sugar bowls saying: NO TITTY DUNKING BY ORDER OF THE MANAGEMENT – cos the young mammies dunk the ends of their tits in so's their bairns'll sook away quiet and they can get on having a smoke and a good fucking ceilidh.

Chell Dinnae scum uz out.

Shuna (*Kay*) So how many is pregnant from your year?

Manda At least seven. Moira Greirson got hers off of Iain Dickinson.

Fionnula The dirty fucking spunker.

Orla *The girls looked at Fionnula –*

Kylah *– who'd famously handjobbed 'The Dick' in front of Moira at the New Year dance.*

Manda Is that a engagement ring, Shoon?

Shuna (*Kay*) Nah, it's just a crappy nothing ring. For protection. The dads from the post-natal try and tap off with the pre-natal mams – so I go 'I'm engaged to a big fucking cunt that'll burst your faces for you' so's they leave me alone. Do you think yous'll win?

Fionnula Fuck the singing, Shu, we're just gonna go mental.

Chell Massive pub crawl –

Orla Check out the shops –

Manda And we'll be back here for the slow dances at the Mantrap.

Fionnula And a couple of hurls roon the bay. Why don't you come the night, Shuna?

Shuna (*Kay*) Ah cannie. Uhm skint. The government going on about us getting up the stick to get single mam's allowance. They've got to be fucking joking. Anyways it was a member of the Her Majesty's fucking Navy that got me in this state.

Orla Can I have a touch?

Shuna (*Kay*) Course, aye.

Michelle helps them put their hands up her Adidas top.

Fionnula Do you get lots of kicks?

Shuna (*Kay*) Oh . . . I tell you . . . it's wild . . . See when you go to Mowat the butcher's – ah go in to get ma mum's mince – the mincer machine it makes the nee-nee noise and the wee thing starts booting away like billy-o.

Fionnula Come on girls, F sharp.

All Neeeeeeeeeeeeee . . .

Chell It's kicking.

Orla That's sooo fucking gorgeous.

Fionnula Condom!

Kylah *Sister Codron.*

Chell Cross between Dracula and Jabba the Hut.

Condom (*Manda, on microphone*) Morning, gurls.

All Morning, Sister Condom.

Condom Bartok, ladies. All together. 'Forth Let the Cattle Roam'.

Fionnula Everybody else gets to sing about love and death – we get to sing about livestock.

They sing from Bartok's 'Enchanted Song'.

Chell On the bus, ladies.

They yell in excitement.

Fionnula Got the goods, girls?

Kylah Two bottles of lemon-flavoured hooch disguised in a bottle of White's lemonade.

Manda Three Bacardi Breezers – off ma sister – in a flask I nicked from ma da.

Chell Large bottle Garvie's American Cream Soda containing eight shots of vodka, four of Cointreau and a little splash of advocaat.

Orla One can of Irn-Bru and a bottle of Metaxa.

Fionnula We'll be fucking stoned before we pass Loch Lomond.

Manda Dinnae start fucking farting on us, Orla.

Orla (*snatching bottle back from Fionnula*) Gimme that. It's alright, I've been cured.

Kylah Of farting?

Orla Of cancer.

Manda That's how it started – in the caravan in Tralee Bay.

All cheer.

Orla I was rushed to fucking A and E I was popping it so much. They put me in a cancer ward and zapped all ma pubes out. Screw the Immac and the Ladyshave, ladies, when you can have chemotherapy.

Kylah But it stopped you farting.

Orla It stopped fucking everything but it didnae work. That's when they put me in the horse piss.

Kay A hospice?

Orla Then they had sponsored run – sent me to fucking Lourdes. And hey presto! I was cured! The pubeless wonder.

Kay So you're a miracle.

Orla Aye, but I never got off with anyone.

Look at the state of us – I could pass for fourteen. There's a lot of lost time to make up for, ladies. I've got two years' worth of pocket money. And a packet of condoms. Let's go mental.

All cheer.

Chell I thought you were saving to go to Lloret de Mar, Orla.

Manda When ma sister went to Lloret de Mar, she got so pissed she puked up over a pedalo then ate a paella that made her diarrhoea so bad she had to stick sanitary towels up her arsehole. It was fucking brilliant.

Chell I'd love to do that.

All We'd all love to do that.

Kylah (*to Kay*) Want some?

Kay No thanks.

Fionnula You do know that this is the party end of the bus.

Kay Yes – I just don't want to be mortal before we even get there.

Fionnula Aye, so you can get another badge for yer blazer. Not everybody wants to go to university with you, Kay Clarke. We've got a whole afternoon in Edinburgh. There's more to life than choir competitions.

Kay Actually I was there last weekend – with my father.

Fionnula Oh, well, this must be a real fucking bore for you.

Kay I can't help who my parents are. I only came up here to be friendly.

Manda And she went off to sit with Fat Clodagh.

Orla What did you have to be like that for?

Kylah She was nearly bustin' with the greets.

Fionnula Fuck her – pluggin' away at her cello on Pulpit Hill – she just wants summat to add on yer UCAS form.

Orla So, Kylah. Hows it going with the band?

Kylah I'm a bit sick of it to tell you the truth.

Orla Really, I'd love to be in a band.

Chell Not wi' fucking Spimmy and those other daft gits.

Orla I think he's quite good looking.

Manda Spimmy?! He's got a fucking mullet.

Fionnula So how come you went with that lot in the first place?

Kylah Well, I was watching the telly.

'Brookside' theme tune. All watch television. They sing the theme tune. Phone rings . . .

Fionnula Would someone answer that fucking phone!

Kylah's Mum (*Chell*) Hello. Oban 2746. Kylah's ma. It's for you.

Kylah Hello? Who is this?

Spimmy (*Fionnula*) Hello. It's Spimmy.

Kylah Who?

Spimmy (*Fionnula*) Spimmy. You don't know me but we heard you singing with the Gaelic League. Will you join our band?

Kylah How did you get my number?

Spimmy (*Fionnula*) You're in the phone book.

Kylah How'd you know my name?

Spimmy (*Fionnula*) It was in the programme. When you sang 'Flowers of the Forest'. It was brilliant.

Kylah But that was Fionnula McConnell.

Spimmy (*Fionnula*) Fuck. We've got the wrong one, Jimmy . . .

Another Voice (*Manda, Drummer*) Fucking ijit. Get off the noo.

Kylah Hang on. Maybe you could meet me anyways.

Kylah Where yous from exactly?

Spimmy (*Fionnula*) Silvermines.

Kylah Not the fucking villages!

What are yous called?

Spimmy (*Fionnula*) Thunderpup.

Kylah Thunderpup?!

Spimmy (*Fionnula*) It's a mixture of 'thunder' and 'pup'. We do a lot of heavy metal.

Kylah You mean I've washed me hair to audition for a band called Thunderpup?

Spimmy (*Fionnula*) Hey, he's got a Fender copy and I can play 'Smoke on the Water'. So what are your influences?

Kylah I dunno. Mostly stuff ma dad had: Judie Tzuke. ELO . . .

Spimmy (*Fionnula*) ELO? You gonna join then?

Kylah Don't you want to hear me sing?

Spimmy (*Fionnula*) We're not that fussy.

Kylah You realise I'm not fucking any of yous. ELO are fucking brilliant. One, two, three, four . . .

They start singing the Electric Light Orchestra's 'Mr Blue Sky'. Over a break in the music:

Manda And you didn't fuck *any* of them?

Kylah Just the bassist, and I wanked the drummer off.

Fionnula Fuckin' hell, Kylah. No wonder they offered you the gig.

Kylah That's what it's like being in a band. The emotions are as important as the music. It's just like being part of a family.

They sing the rest of 'Mr Blue Sky'.

Manda Piss stop!

Orla Hurry up, I'm fucking burstin!

Chell The Ladies is full. Or –

Fionnula In the Gents, gurls.

Orla Let me go first – it's an emergency.

She goes into the cubicle.

Look at the fucking seat. I'm no sitting on that.

Manda Here.

Orla What is it?

Manda A sandwich.

Orla What am I supposed to do with that?

Manda Put a slice under each leg.

Orla I'm no sitting on a cucumber sandwich. I'll just have ti squat over it.

Piiiiiissssssssssssssssssssssssssssss . . .

Kylah (*also boistin'*) Hurry up, for Christ's sake.

The piss stops. Then starts again. Then drip, drips. Then Orla comes out. Kylah rushes in.

Chell In comes some American twat with tartan pants and orthopaedic trainers.

American Gadgie (*Kay*) Apologies, I thought this was the Gentlemen's comfort station.

Fionnula It is but the Lassies' was full. Don't mind us, mister. We're good Catholic schoolgirls.

Kylah Fuck fuck fucking fuck.

American Gadgie (*Kay*) Are you sure she's alright in there?

Kylah You've used all the bog paper, you skinny fucking witch.

Orla Use the other fucking sandwich. It's on the back there.

Kylah I'm not stuffing a cucumber sandwich up my snatch for anybody.

American Gadgie (*Kay*) Are you sure there's nothing I can do to help?

Orla You couldnae get us a couple more hooches, could you?

Back on the bus:

Chell Did you know, right, that my sister is also my auntie.

Kylah How's that?

Chell Well, ma first dad was drowned, right. They never found his body so there was no funeral or nothing. We just kept his shaving things above the sink in case he was stranded on an inlet. Then ma mam married Daddy MacDougal. Who we *call* Dad. Though actually my real dad wasn't really my real dad – he was just a sailor who fucked off.

Orla I'm not sure I'm following this.

Chell Anyway, ma sister Shirley got pregnant last summer off Mad Buzz MacDougal.

Fionnula The beekeeper?

Chell Who is Daddy Patrick's younger brother. So my sister is also my auntie.

Manda Buzz MacDougal up by Tulloch Ferry?

Fionnula He's a right cunt.

Chell I know. Once I found three puppies up there whats mammy had died by the Ferry and I fed them with a pippet.

Orla A what?

Chell A pippet. A fucking squeegy thing, like an eye-dropper. I kept them in a big cardboard box and I used to heat this big stone up in the fire and put it in their box covered in an old sweater and they would all be curled up there on the gone-cold-ness of the stone.

All Aaah.

Chell Aye, but then I got the alarm clock from the spare room and wrapped it up and put it in the box cos they like the ticking cos it's like their mammy's heart. But the hotness of the stone shattered the glass of the alarm clock and in the morning all the puppies were bled to death, covered in blood and shit and everything.

Fionnula Ooh, that's awful.

Manda You've had a lot of death to deal with.

Chell I know.

Orla Jesus fucking shite!

Look at that!

Fionnula What?

Orla In the window.

Fionnula For Christ's sake. That girl is having it off with yon big fella. Jesus fuck. You can see her wee bottom segments heaving up and down.

Orla Christ, the dirty hoor's having a look at wi.

The girls wave.

Manda Go for it, sister.

Chell If the city girls are all like that there's not much hope for us this afternoon.

Condom (*Kay, on microphone*) What on earth is going on back there?

Orla We just saw some dirty Edinburgh lassie having intercoursing sex with a fat fella. And we were waving at her.

Fionnula She didn't actually say that. She said . . .

Orla Nothing, sister.

Condom (*Kay, on microphone*) Listen carefully, ladies. You must be in school uniform, without make-up or piercings of any kind, Chell MacDougal, by six o'clock in the Conference for the practice. The Thirds will be first then the Seconds will be second. The Firsts will be last. There's a message in there somewhere. And remember, not only are you representing Our Ladies, the entire Port, but also God himself. God, I tell you. Anybody late will pay with their scalps. Any questions?

Orla Did you see any submariners down the town this morning, Sister?

Chell McDonald's!

All (*except Kay*) McDonald's!

Fionnula And we all got off the bus. Kay Clarke went off by herself somewhere. Me, Orla, Kylah, Manda and Chell, Manda went to McDonald's.

Kylah A Big Mac, large fries, and a Coke.

Fionnula A double cheeseburger and a chocolate shake.

Manda A Quarter Pounder, large fries and a vanilla shake.

Chell Barbie Happy Meal.

Orla Two double cheeseburgers, large fries, chocolate cake, a coffee and a hot fudge sundae and a milkshake.

As they eat their McDonald's:

Chell Once, right, I knew this lass who was going out with a farmer's son from Loch Nell and he'd gave her mam a fucking live turkey for Christmas – they didnae know what to do wi' it so they had it in the back room just running all about the carpets and everything. Anyways, they got pissed Christmas Eve, caught the fucker but didn't have the guts to chop its heed off so they gassed it, plucked it, and were gonna stuff it when the bastard woke up on the chopping board and went fucking mental – so they decided to give it back to the farmer laddie but it escaped at the bus stop and was running around the port all naked wi' ne feathers on it.

Fionnula If it was nae on the table by lunchtime it was cos somebody was shagging it.

The girls laugh.

OK. So what you wearing tonight, Kye?

Kylah Well, I was thinking, ma silver shirt, top three buttons open and my light-coloured stretchpants – those shiny ones that flare out at the feet with the little pockets here and the side zips and with the black strappyish sandals, tan toe-nail varnish, ma hair slicked back and glossed with a parting and tan eyeshadow, a wee sliver of silver cross top of the eyelids here, lighter on the bottom, then a coat of black under that, mascara and dark colour lip-liner, tan lipstick to go with ma nails an' toes then a listery lip-gloss on top.

Fionnula Cool.

Kylah Well, I'm no wearing that. I thought I'd wear ma hair down wi that skirt ah got from the catalogue.

Chell My Uncle Buzz used to fill pillows with his own hair.

Fionnula *We all looked at Chell.*

Handel's 'My heart is inditing' goes over the next sequence.

All five girls squeeze into the toilet, remove clothes from coloured Nike and Adidas bags, shoes from Superstore carriers, deodorant – it's all amazingly orchestrated as it's such a tiny place, deadly seriousness of it all. Each girl comes out of the cubicle and describes what she's wearing.

Fionnula *French connection, viscose, long sleeved, blue-stripped shirt. Black A-line skirt, open-laced platforms, Wonderbra, cotton knickers.*

Kylah *Lilac T-shirt, denim mini-skirt, high-heeled sandals, bra an' knickers.*

Chell *Leopard-print short-sleeved top, short cream skirt, cut on the bias, cheap suede boots, leopardskin tanga, with matching bra.*

Manda *School shirt open to show her sister's Wonderbra, blue, pleated skirt, plasticky shoes and sister's G-string.*

Orla *Crushed velvet body-top wi' thin straps and lacey shirt. Flared hipster trousers from the catalogue. School shoes, no bra needed. Brand new black G-string.*

Each girl is jeered on by the others. They all cheer Orla.

Fionnula What we gonna do with our uniforms?

Chell Put them all in here.

Let's get go fucking mental.

> *Start of 'Long Black Road' by the Electric Light Orchestra.*

Orla Five lemon Hooches, please.

Gadgie (*Kay*) Sorry, ladies, you can't eat them in here.

Kylah What?

Gadgie (*Kay*) No food, girls. We've got a menu.

Chell It isn't food. It's a fucking Magnum lolly.

Fionnula I'll give you a lick if you want.

Gadgie (*Kay*) Less of your lip.

Chell What a miserable cunt. I thought it was supposed to be Happy Hour.

Gadgie Look, I'm just doing my job.

Kylah Keep your fucking hair on – it's alright.

We'd like to see your cock . . . tail list.

Chell I nearly cracked ma shite.

A'm nearly cracking ma fucking shite at you!

Kylah Mmm I like a nice *cock*-tail. Have you got a liquidiser? That you can stick yer *cock*-tails in?

Chell Ahm actually doing it. I'm actually cracking ma fucking shite.

Kylah Well, stick these in wi' a bit a cream, Southern Comfort.

Fionnula And we'll have an ashtray.

Chell And five shots of Sambuca – while we're waiting. A'm just goin' for a wazz.

A guy approaches.

Guy (*Chell*) Hello, gurls. Do yous know you have two hundred and six bones in your body? If you play your cards right the neet, you can have one more.

Fionnula Look, fuck off, we're trying to drink our Hooches.

Guy (*Chell*) Whoa, lady, it's just a wee bit o' banter – most of the lads in here go 'Ma dick just died, can I bury it in your arse?'

Manda Just fuck off or we'll glass ye, you illiterate cunt.

Orla Steady on, Manda, he was pretty cute.

Manda It's the first pub, Orla, if we start hitting on boys the noo there'll be a queue of butchers' dogs ahind us by five o'clock.

Chell is wrapping the holes on the filter of her ciggie with a Rizla.

Kylah What are you doing?

Chell I'm wrapping the holes on the filters.

Kylah Why ya don't just buy stronger cigarettes?

Chell It works out a wee bit cheaper.

Kylah Fuck that. I'm getting some red Marlboro.

She gets off the stool with difficulty and walks to the machine.

Fionnula You shouldnae be smoking them.

Look at Yolanda McCormack. Afore ye joined she used to be a soprano.

Kylah Never!

Fionnula Guide's honour, she used to smoke Silk Cut Extra Mild till the French exchange: came back on the Gitanes now she sings bass with Fat Clodagh.

Kylah Fuck that. It makes yer voice sexy.

Kylah puts money in, the fags drop from one hand to another but so low that Kylah will have to bend down. She tries several times but realises she will reveal herself to the ogling guys. She goes back to Chell.

Oh shit. Chell.

Chell What is it?

Kylah Ma fucking skirt's too tight to bend down and get them out. Give it a go.

Chell No way José – I'm not showing ma fanny for free in here.

Gadgie Five Sambucas, ladies.

Fionnula Excuse me, my friend's got a problem with the cigarette machine.

Gadgie (*Kay*) How much did she put in?

Kylah Oh, it's not that, it's just our skirts are so tight we cannae get our Marlboros without gross public indecency. You couldn't lift them out for me could you?

He assists.

There was this girl up our way got pregnant from the guy who fills the cigarette machines.

Chell Thirteen, she was. Back of the van up against the Lambert and Butler. Had her wee baby and ah hear, subsequently, it became a heavy smoker.

They all laugh, uproariously.

Gadgie (*Kay*) Look, girls, keep it down, girls. My manager's getting jumpy.

Chell Fuck that: Sambuca challenge.

All of this is interlaced with 'Long Black Road' by the Electric Light Orchestra.

Right, you knock it back – stick a match in and Bob's your uncle.

Manda We'll fucking die.

Fionnula Don't hold it in too long.

Manda What? Are you sure about this.

Lights snap out, they each take the Sambuca challenge: blue/purple flames. They all cheer uproariously.

Fuck!

Orla Five more Sambucas!

Gadgie (*Kay*) I'm sorry – but I'm gonna have to ask you, ladies, not light them.

Orla Fuck that. We paid for them.

Manda Is it no our business how we drink them?

Gadgie (*Kay*) Look . . . I never asked you for ID, did I?

Chell You're saying you'll serve us even though you think we're under age, but only if we drink certain liquids?

Gadgie (*Kay*) All I am asking is that you just go easy on the pyromania. There was a girl in Dirty Dick's scorched her throat and it swole up her whole oesophagus.

Fionnula A dirty dick swole her what?

They piss themselves laughing.

Orla Did she die?

Gadgie (*Kay*) Well, she wasn't feeling too smart.

Fionnula Look, mister. We paid for these drinks. We'll suck them up our arseholes if we want to.

Chell Watch this.

She knocks back all the shots then blows a huge fire flame.

Fionnula Hot fucking shite!

They sing a riotous end to 'Long Black Road', then:

Gadgie (*Kay*) Right. Out. The fucking lot of yous.

Chell Fuck. I think I've singed ma eyebrow.

Orla Who's coming to Schuh?

Manda I will.

Orla Ky?

Kylah I've got to go buy CDs for Spimmy and the lads. They've given me a load of money.

Orla Chell?

Chell No, I think I'll go with Kylah to HIV.

Fionnula MV. You stupid cow.

Orla Fionnulla?

Fionnula I don't want to spend me one afternoon in the Capital watching yous two try on Doc Martins.

Orla Where we'z gonna meet then?

Kylah The Pill Box. It's a really cool bar on the corner of the Grassmarket.

Orla The Pill Box. At half past. OK? See yous.

Orla and Manda go off.

Kylah You coming?

Fionnula *Then for some reason I said:*

No, I think I'll just go have a dander.

Kylah What? By yerself?

Fionnula Aye, I'll catch yous up at the Pill Box.

Kylah *And off she went. On her own.*

What's up wi' her?

Chell I dunno but she's getting right on my tits. Lady Muck. Did ye hear her wi Kay Clarke, who the fuck does she think she is?

Orla Whatdya think?

Manda Aye, they look great as well.

Orla You no think ah look like a skinny drug addict or something?

Manda A little bit but you look cool.

Orla Don't you want to try some?

Manda I can't, Orla. I've no been getting ma allowance since ma da went on the dole.

I know it sounds shit and everything but I've worked out different strategies to cope and everything.

Orla What d'ya mean?

Manda Like Cleopatra baths.

Orla What do you mean, Cleopatra baths?

Manda When I get depressed I sneak in the bathroom and put two scoops of powered milk in when I fill the bath up and just lie there like I'm Cleopatra. Off *Carry On.*

34

Orla Isn't it sticky?

Manda No, you should try it. My dad slips in after. I pretend I don't know. But it saves him putting back on the immersion.

Orla Right I'm going to take these. And a pair of those in size six.

Manda What you doing?

Orla I'm getting you them.

Manda No, you can't do that.

Orla Ah want you to have them.

Manda No, Orla, no ways – that's your cancer money that.

Orla I'm getting them whether you like it or not.

Manda Thank you, Orla. That's the nicest thing that anyone's ever done for me.

And then I hugged her. And she was cold. Like a bag of bones.

Nowt there.

I love you, Orla.

   Meanwhile:

Chell Fucking hell, there must be a hundred quid.

Kylah I know.

Chell What they fucking spending a hundred quid on Status Quo and Hawkwind for?

Kylah I know, what a right heap of shite.

Chell I dunno what you hang around that bunch of idiots for.

Kylah But that's what I want to do. Music. I've got a job starting in September.

Chell Whereabouts?

Kylah On the record counter at Woolies!

Chell Don't set your sights too high.

Kylah You've got to start somewhere.

Chell I think you should dump them.

Kylah Spimmy?

Chell Aye, the lot of them. What you going round with a twat with a mullet for? Screw Woolworths. Go solo, move to fucking Glasgow. You could be like Sharleen Spiteri, Ky.

Kylah But she's in a band.

Chell I didn't mean literally. I mean world-famous. Fuck the CDs. Who cares about that shite if you're leaving the band? I'll tell you what you need.

Kylah Wha?

Chell A pub with a phone.

The pub with a phone:

Kylah Have you a phone book, please?

Regular (*Orla*) Are yous trying to give us all heart attacks with those skirts?

Chell Where's your phone, please?

Regular (*Kay*) None of us will sleep the night.

Regular (*Fionnula*) Don't have one.

Chell How come you've got a phone book but you haven't got a phone?

Barman (*Manda*) It was there till Saturday. Some lad walked out with the handset in his jacket.

Regular (*Fionnula*) That's nothing, Chugg. I woke up in the armchair Saturday with a defrosted haddock in ma pocket.

Chell But hang on, you've a phone there.

Regular (*Orla*) That's for regulars.

Chell An' how much do you huff to drink to become a regular?

Kylah Have you got Sambuca?

Barman (*Kay*) Some what?

Chell Two double vodka and Cokes.

And we'll have the phone, please. It's an emergency.

Barman (*Fionnula*) Where are yous phoning then?

Chell Australia.

Kylah Oban. I'm leaving ma band.

Regular (*Manda*) Are you in a band?

Chell We're all in a choir.

Regular (*Kay*) Do you play dominoes as well?

The Regulars all laugh.

Kylah Hello. It's Kylah, Missus Greig. (Kay blah blah.) Aye. Fine aye. Is Spimmy there? (Kay blah blah.) Spimmy, it's me . . . Look there's something ah need to tell you. A'm leaving the band.

Fionnula as Spimmy on mic, incoherent phone noises.

Chell What's he saying?

Kylah Shush. . . . No, it's nothing to do wi the drum solo . . . A'm just no enjoying it . . .

Regular (*Orla*) You tell him, lassie.

Fionnula as Spimmy. Phone noises again.

Kylah What? Nut-nut, What do you mean, sack them?

Chell What's he saying now, for God's sake?

Kylah He says do ah want to get rid of the drummer and bass player?

Chell What an arsehole.

Fionnula as Spimmy on phone again.

Kylah No, it's got nothing to do with it. Anyways, I only wanked him off the once.

The Regulars nearly choke on their drink.

Chell Tell him he's a cheeky fucking get and it's none of his business.

Fionnula as Spimmy on phone again.

Kylah That's Chell MacDougal – you met her when we played the High School.

Fionnula as Spimmy.

Chell What's he saying?

Kylah He says you're a pikey tinker?

Chell grabs the phone.

All Regulars Uh-oh.

Chell I'll fuckin' brain you – go an' pluck your one-string banjo, you wee short dick cunt.

Regular (*Manda*) Don't break that phone.

Spimmy is going mental in his squeaky voice.

Kylah Look, calm down.

Barman (*Manda*) Is he still giving you grief?
Cm'ere.

The Barman takes the phone.

Listen here – the lassie fucking telt you, she's left yur
band, so go an' fuck yourself and watch what your
fucking well saying. Who am I? I'm her new fucking
manager.

Cheers from the Regulars.

Aye, record contracts the lot – who the fuck are you,
Opportunity fuckin' Knocks? She's been doon in this
city . . . (*Mouths 'How long?'*)

Kylah Since this morning.

Barman (*Manda*) She's doon in this city just the morn
and she's got a new manager and a record contract, and
all the fucking rest of it – so think about that, son, you
little chavvy cunt, one more word outa ye and I'll be up
to fucking Oban and snap your frigging neck for you.

He gives the phone back.

There you go, pet.

Kylah Bye.

Chell What we gonna do now?

All Spend their fucking money.

Meanwhile:

Orla Can I ask ye a question?

Manda What sort of question.

Orla Well, will you promise not to say anything to anyone else?

Manda I suppose so.

Orla What does it taste like?

Manda What taste like?

Orla You know . . . spunk . . . jizz . . . cum.

Manda Have you never tasted it?

Orla I pretended to but I've never really done it with anybody. I'm a bit behind cos of ma cancer.

Manda It's a bit like snot only warmer.

Orla How warm?

Manda Ah saw steam come off it once behind the Mantrap. But mind, it was fucking freezing. So have you never done it with anybody?

Orla Not properly. There was once in the hospital. When I was having my radiotherapy. I was on this mixed corridor. And I used to see this bloke who was in there dying too – he was ancient, like thirty or something. He was from Norway or Finland or somewhere.

And when I went to go for a piss I'd see his room and he was lying there morphine drips in his arms and everything. He was a sailor or something. You could see the tattoos. Sometimes when it was quiet ah could hear it pop-popping, next door, all his internal juices inside of him, digesting him alive. And he would say stuff in Swedish. Nobody could understand him but I knew what he was saying: looking up at God, saying 'Take me now, you fucking bastard, why don't you fucking take me now?' Then there was this one night. I could hear him so I sneaked along the corridor in a nightie. And I went into his room and closed the door so no one would see. And I just stood there listening to him gurgling. Then I, don't know why I did, I put ma hand out and touched his bag of piss and it was hot and I followed the tube down with ma fingers, under the blanket, till it reached his cock. And he was just, like, lying there and I thought – I'll be like you soon. So I was stood there holding his cock and then I lifted up his balls – you know to check he hadn't shit himself – and it was fine – so I took the tube out of the end of his cock and I got up on the bed – then I thought, fuck, if I put ma weight on him I might kill him. So I decided to like hover over him.

I had one hand up like this to keep balanced and I reached back to like grab his knob to push it in – but it just flipped from side to side like a dead fish – and I was shaking, I don't know if it was turned on-ness of fear and I was trying to force it up. And then I realised – that this wasn't about me. That I was there and he was going to die and I'm getting all the satisfaction and I thought no, this is all the wrong way round, this should be my gift to *him*.

And so I thought I would suck him off. So I turned round and I put it in my mouth and I sucked and sucked but it still wasn't hard so I gave him a bit of a wank – like it said in *More*. And I was looking at the door terrified that the night sister would come in. So I did it faster and faster and I could feel it getting stiff in my hand, and he started shouting something up my arse in Swedish. And I was wanking him and wanking him. The fuck – all of a sudden he spunked up. It was fucking everywhere. And I was wiping it off and he was slavvering. So I tried to find something to clean it up.

Then – he sits up.

Aghh!

Then he started to come towards me. Like something out of *Frankenstein*.

41

And he was pulling all of his drips out. And the alarms went off.

And he was coming right at me, so I hit him, with my two hands like. And he fell down on the floor.

Fuck, fuck.

And then he shat himself, and he pissed all over.

And I looked at him flailing about in the skitter and the piss. And I didn't know what to do. So I just held him there. Naked. Shrivelled up like a fossil. And I was crying. And all I could say was: 'Sorry, sorry, I'm so so sorry.'

The next day they'd tied him to the bed. With big belts.

Fionnula This one's for Orla.

They sing a song for Orla. Possibly 'For You' by Judie Tzuke.

Pill Box!

Orla In the name of God.

Manda What a gormless bunch of bampots.

Kylah You made it!

Chell We're fucking plastered. Kylah left the band and we've already drunk half of their CD money.

Kylah It's fucking lush. They've got karaoke. Chell's put her name down!

Orla OK, I'll get some drinks.

Two pints of cider, please.

Chopper (*Manda*) Excuse me – I really like your boots.

Orla Oh?! Thanks. I just bought them.

Chopper (*Manda*) I don't think I've ever seen you in here before.

Orla No. We're from Oban. We're just here to meet up with our pals. We're going mental. It's the choir competition.

Chopper Oh aye.

Orla What's that?

Chopper (*Manda*) It's a budgie.

Orla A budgie?! Why have you brought it into a karaoke bar?

Chopper (*Manda*) I'm looking after it for the man.

Careful, you're spilling that all over.

Orla It's a very liquidy drink, cider.

Chopper (*Manda*) Here. I'll help you.

Chell has come over to protect Orla. She grabs the drinks off Chopper.

Chell No you don't.

Chopper (*Manda*) Is this one your pals?

Chell Actually, I'm her mam. Fuck off, you little charver.

Chopper (*Manda*) I was only trying to be helpful.

Chell I'm warning you, piss off and leave her alone.

Chopper goes off.

Orla He was quite nice, Chell.

Chell Jesus Christ, Orla. He's a fucking retard. Was that a budgie cage?!

Meanwhile:

Fionnula It was the first time I'd been to Edinburgh. It was the first time I'd been anywhere. And I was excited. Like secretly excited about being on my own. I was never on my own. I was always wi' somebody.

But now I was in all these auld streets, just going up alleys, weaving through passages and that, and then I saw her.

She looked older, cooler on her own. And she'd changed from her uniform.

She had like this suede skirt and boots and I don't really know why but I started to follow her, you know, like in a film, stepping in doorways, hiding behind cars and that. Staying enough behind just so she wouldn't see me. And I was just a few steps behind her and she went into this wine bar, this dead posh wine bar – and I stood there looking in – I never knew there were places that posh in Scotland – and I hovered outside – just looking – and I thought fuck it – I'm going in . . .

Back in the Pill Box:

Barman (*Kay*) Next on karaoke we've got a lass from Oban – Chell MacDougal!

Chell does a karaoke version of 'Sweet Talking Woman' by the Electric Light Orchestra. All the girls cheer.

Chell Then this guy in a suit appeared.

Suit (*Fionnula*) Hi girls.

Manda Who's this, fucking Bryan Ferry?

Suit (*Fionnula*) You're no Jim Clarke's wee sister, are you?

Kylah No. And neither are we.

Suit (*Fionnula*) You gurls celebrating?

44

Kylah We will when you're gone.

Suit (*Fionnula*) This is Mike, he's been staying with me since his divorce.

Divorcee (*Kay*) Hello.

Suit (*Fionnula*) Fucking hell, Mike, put a bit a spark in it. Did you know you have two hundred and six bones –

Kylah What a cursèd nuisance.

Look. We're not interested in yer patter – we're on a school trip – and we're only shagging people born in the twentieth century.

Chell Steady on, Ky. I quite fancied him.

Kylah Jesus, Chell, it'd be like shagging Mr Eldon.

Suit (*Fionnula*) So this school you go to, is it an all-girls' school?

Chell Aye, it's a convent wi' nuns and all that.

Manda They call it the Virgin Megastore.

Chell In total. We've had sixteen pregnant since last September. Seven in our year.

Suit (*Fionnula*) Jesus Christ.

Chell There was one lassie pregnant before her confirmation off a guy who fills up cigarette machines.

Suit (*Fionnula*) Dirty bastard.

Manda The last school disco we got a drug raid from the police.

Suit (*Fionnula*) I think I might have died and gone to heaven. Listen, we just live across the road there. Do you gurls want to come over for a drink?

Orla What's he saying?

Manda He says do we want to go over to his place for a drink?

Kylah You're joking, aren't you?

Chell Come on, Ky. It might be a laugh.

Kylah *Then this weird bloke says:*

Danny (*Orla*) Can I tag along?

Kylah Who the fuck is *he*?

All That's Danny.

Suit (*Fionnula*) Look, Danny, we're on the pull here.

Danny (*Orla*) Just for a bit. I'll keep out your way.

Suit (*Fionnula*) As long as you behave yourself. Don't let him carry the bags.

Chopper (*Manda, to Orla*) Excuse me. I wondered if I could have the pleasure of the next dance?

Orla With me?

Chopper (*Manda*) Yes.

Orla Are you sure?

Chell Are you coming or what?

Orla I think I'll stay here, actually.

Chopper (*Manda*) I really like your 'atmosphere'.

Orla What do you mean, you really like my atmosphere?

Chopper (*Manda*) I normally wear glasses but I look like a prick in them.

Orla What, you mean you can't see what I look like.

Chopper (*Manda*) Only vaguely.

Orla Look, I don't mind people with glasses. Why don't you put them on.

Chopper (*Manda*) OK, but don't laugh, mind. Wow. You're fucking lush.

Orla So are you.

Chopper (*Manda*) My name's Chopper.

Orla Chopper?!

Chopper (*Manda*) Cos of my bike. Can I kiss you?

Orla I thought you'd never ask.

They dance awkwardly and the scene changes to a posh wine bar.

Fionnula Kay?!

Kay Fionnula!

Fionnula Fancy seeing you here.

Kay I thought you were with the others.

Fionnula No, I just thought I'd pop out for a quiet drink, somewhere sophisticated.

She fails to get on the stool properly.

Barmaid (*Chell*) What can I get you?

Fionnula What flavours of Hooch d'ya have?

Barmaid (*Chell*) I'm afraid we don't stock Hooch.

Fionnula What's that?

Kay G and T. Do you want one?

Fionnula Aye, I think I better.

Kay Can we have two gin and tonics.

Fionnula Make them stiff ones. Talking of stiff ones, what about that girl and the fat lad, eh? I thought Orla was goan' wet hersel'.

Kay I like Orla.

Fionnula Aye, she's just got very low expectations. She's never even been for a Chinese, you know. That's how it is out in the villages. Not very sophisticated.

The gins arrive.

Up yer bum.

I see you got changed as well.

Kay It's not just you lot that can get done up, you know, actually it's because I was looking at a house. For when I come to uni in September. I can't wait for freshers' week.

Fionnula What's that?

Kay When you go to uni they have a whole week for parties. You could easily get to uni, Fionnula.

Fionnula Coming out wi' thousands of pounds of debts and shit.

Kay What are you going to do? Stay in the Port?

Fionnula Who says a'm staying in the Port?

Look, you don't know anything about me, up there in your house on Pulpit Hill plugging away at yer cello. An' ah suppose you'll be off backpacking around the Himalayas wi your daddy's credit card.

Kay In my dreams. I couldn't have a cigarette, could I?

Fionnula Kay Clarke!

Kay I'm not as stuck-up as you think, you know.

Fionnula Have you ever tried tequila?

Kay Do you set fire to it?

Fionnula No. Nothing weird like that. You put salt on your hand, lick it, neck the tequila and you bite a slice lemon. It tastes like shite. But it gets you mashed as anything.

Kay OK, well, let's try some.

Fionnula Three tequila slammers – each – six in total. And two bottles of Corona – to take the taste away.

Kay Are you sure about this?

Chell comes on with a tray of slammers. They 'do' the slammers – Kay is instantly pissed and Fionnula more poised.

Once, right, my mam and dad had a fancy dress party and the consultant gynaecologist came as Goldfinger. From James Bond. Get it. Goldfinger.

Fionnula Are you alright with those gin and tonics? Ya dinnae think of doctors having a sense of humour.

Kay That's nothing, when Dad was at med school and one of the students cut a man's cock off during a dissection, an' they put it on a thread and went on a bus and this student doctor put it down his trouser leg so the end was jiggling out the bottom on the piece of string.

Fionnula Are you gonna be a doctor?

Kay Lawyer.

Fionnula Well, you dinnae need qualifications to get knobs out on buses round the Port – Manda's done it on most routes in Argyll.

Kay What's Manda gonna do when she leaves?

Fionnula Get pregnant to a guy up the Complex, have a wee boy wi' a skinhead an' an earring called Shane.

Kay Do you know her sister?

Fionnula 'Ma big sister – Catriona.' If I hear her mention her again I swear I'll put her eyes out. She's always

49

bragging about boys and that, but you know she never sleeps with them – most she does is handjobs round the back of the Mantrap. She's going 'I've been wi' him an' him' but she just means they've ruined one of her tops.

Kay I think she's just insecure.

Fionnula We're all insecure.

Kay But you're the most popular girl at school. What are you insecure about?

Fionnula Dunno. What I am, where a'm going.

Kay Everybody thinks about that.

Fionnula But in a bigger way. I mean life is full of possibilities. And most of the possibilities just get left. We're just a tiny percentage of what we could have been. No matter who you are you go through life and you never do what you could have done. Most of your life is left unlived.

Kay I'm not sure I am really following this.

Fionnula Haven't you ever just done something just to see what would happen?

Kay I went to bed with Iain Dickinson.

Fionnula The Dick?! Fuck. No. When?

Kay About nine weeks ago.

Fionnula But ah mean, what, how do you even know him?

Kay Ah don't. I was with Anna Bessie's brother out at the Barns then his car broke down so I got a lift back with Catriona.

Fionnula Manda's sister?!

Kay And Iain Dickinson was in the car.

Then we went back to her flat. We were playing this

game and you had to pass vodka round: mouth to mouth – so I started snogging him.

Fionnula Jesus Christ.

Kay And then I snogged Catriona too.

Fionnula Fucking hell!

Kay And then before I knew it we were all in bed together.

Fionnula What, you went to bed with Manda's sister?!

Kay You think I'm disgusting, don't you?

Fionnula Fucking hell, Kay!

And did you, you know, *fuck* her too?

Kay I was as mashed as anything.

Fionnula Two Bloody Marys.

Fuck. But would you, you know, do it again – wi' a girl?

Kay I dunno – I don't think I'm a lesbian or anything – I mean I didn't really know what I was doing. You think I'm a dirty perv, don't you?

Fionnula No. I once got off with this lad in France just cos he looked like a girl, actually.

And ah sort of realised ah think ah like girls as much as boys.

Kay What are you saying, Fionnula?

Fionnula Maybe more. Kay, I think you are a very attractive young woman.

Kay What?!

Fionnula snogs Kay sitting on the stool. The impassioned clinch forces Kay to her feet – at which point she instantly crumples.

Fionnula Oh shite.

Barmaid (*Chell*) What did you do to her?

Fionnula Kay – wake up. Wake up!

Barmaid (*Chell*) I better call an ambulance.

Fionnula Oh no, you cannae – ah mean we need to be up at the conference centre at six o'clock . . . Kay . . .

Barmaid (*Chell*) I take it you'll not be needing the Bloody Marys.

Fionnula No. I'll have them.

Chell and Manda go into the Suit's flat.

Suit (*Fionnula*) This is the gaff.

Alright there, Danny?

Put the bags down in here, now sit there and keep quiet. Let's get this party into gear.

What do you want to drink, ladies?

Manda Do you have peach schnapps?

Suit (*Fionnula*) We've got two crates of lager in the fridge.

Chell OK, we'll have those.

Kylah So how long have you been divorced?

Suit (*Fionnula*) Don't get him started.

Divorcee (*Kay*) Do you want to see a picture of ma wife?

Chell Your ex-wife.

Divorcee (*Kay*) Here you go.

Kylah Aww, is that you on your wedding day?

Divorcee (*Kay*) Aye.

Kylah Your wife was gorgeous.

Divorcee (*Kay*) Aye. She was.

Manda What's her name?

Divorcee (*Kay*) Ailish.

Kylah Look, Manda, his ex-wife was really really pretty. How come yous split?

Divorcee (*Kay*) It was sort of incompatible personalities.

Suit (*Fionnula*) Aye, she hated your fuckin' guts – c'mon, man, get wi' the programme here. Make yourself at home, girls, I'm just gonna change into something more comfortable.

He leaves.

Chell So how long were you together?

Divorcee (*Kay*) Five year. Do you wanna see a video? Of the wedding?

Manda Not really.

Divorcee (*Kay*) Just hang on a minute.

He gets the video.

Chell Christ, these two are as much fun as a day in the morgue.

Manda Danny, you might be our man yet!

The Divorcee is back.

Divorcee (*Kay*) Look, here it is. There's Ailish. Now watch this bit. That's ya man there, you wouldn't recognise him would you? And there's me.

Suit (*Fionnula, from his room*) What the fuck are you putting that on for?

Divorcee (*Kay*) And this is Ailish.

Suit (*Fionnula*) Turn it off, you fucking idiot.

Manda She looks gorgeous.

Divorcee (*Kay*) And here's the kiss.

Suit (*Fionnula*) Don't let him rewind it.

Divorcee (*Kay*) I'll just rewind it.

He rewinds.

What a fucking idiot.

He bursts into tears

What a total fucking idiot.

Chell Are you OK?

Divorcee (*Kay*) No, I'm not OK. I ruined everything.

Suit (*Fionnula, off*) What the fuck's going on out there?

Manda He burst out wi' the greets and locked himself in the bog.

Suit (*Fionnula, off*) Didn't think that would take long.

Kylah Look, come out. It's alright. We've turned it off.

Suit (*Fionnula, off*) Just leave him. He'll be in there for hours.

Manda This is fucking rubbish. Let's get out of here.

Chell I can't believe he's locked himself in there, I'm dying for a piss.

Suit (*Fionnula*) Forget him, girls, he'll be in there for hours. Get yourselves in here!

Manda and Chell push the door open. Suit man is stark naked standing on his head with an enormous erection and blue ink under his armpits.

Chell Fucking hell, that's some joint yu've goat on ya.

Manda What's that stuff under yer arms?

Suit (*Fionnula*) It's the ink from squids, rub it in an' you can keep a hard-on all day. C'mon, ladies, yon cunt'll be in there hours. Whoaaa!!

Kylah *Then suddenly he fell over and gashed himself on a mountain bike.*

Suit (*Fionnula*) Aaaarrggh. Fuck fuck, I've cut me bloody toe off.

Manda We'll phone you an ambulance.

Suit (*Fionnula*) Nah, fuck that, I'll get a taxi. The phone.

He phones taxi.

A taxi – to the hospital. Over the road from the Pill Box. Aye – I'm ready the noo.

Kylah (*to the Divorcee*) Listen, your pal's had an accident and he's cut most of his toe off.

Suit (*Fionnula*) Get out here and shag these lassies, you stupid cunt, they're beautiful wi' pierced eyebrows an Christ knows what an they're here in our house the now.

Chell Just you watch yur mouth, Hopalong.

Manda Look you're goan' have to get over this sometime an' yur mate has really cut his toe bad.

Chell And I'm burstin'.

Door buzzer goes.

Suit (*Fionnula*) Get that.

Manda Hello.

Buzzer (*Orla*) Did you order a taxi?

Manda Aye – just coming. Dunno his name but you'll recognise him by his cut toe.

Buzzer (*Orla*) I'm not taking anyone with a cut toe.

Manda He says he's not taking anyone with a cut toe.

Suit (*Fionnula*) Fucking dosser. Tell him I'll do a shite on his taxi floor.

Manda He says he's just coming and it's just a graze.

Suit (*Fionnula*) Come on – who's comin with uz?

Kylah We're not going anywhere – we've got to meet our pals.

Suit (*Fionnula*) You slags.

Kylah I'll be glad to get back the Port. Least you can get a snog off of someone who's no gonna knife ya.

Chell I'm fucking burstin' here, Manda.

Manda Hi, Chell needs in to go to toilet.

Divorcee (*Kay*) I'm no coming out till Ailish comes home.

Chell Tell him a'm gonna pee ma pants.

Manda Look, this is an emergency.

Divorcee (*Kay*) A'm not coming out for anything.

Chell What 'ma gonna do?

Manda I think you'll have to do a Fionnula and go in the sink.

Chell What about the dishes?

Manda Well, I'm no goan' do them.

Chell Shut the door. I don't want that Danny burstin' in.

Fuck, there's half a sausage roll in there.

Manda Hurry up.

Chell There. Is there any kitchen towel?

Manda In this place?! You've got to be joking. I've got some hankies in ma bag.

Fuck.

Chell What?

Manda Fuck. Fucking bastard's robbed our stuff.

Chell Who?

Manda Danny.

Chell What? He's took the bags?

Manda No. He's left the bags. He's fucked off with wer uniforms.

Chell Jesus Christ. Condom'll go mental.

Manda He's left a note: 'Thank you for the uniforms. Think of me as I wank on them evry night.' Spelt e-v-r-y.

Chell Thick cunt.

Manda There he is, he's got your knickers on his heed.

Chell Oh fucking hell!

Divorcee (*Kay*) Ailish . . . Ailish . . .

They start singing 'Don't Bring Me Down', which is interweaved throughout the next section.

The hospital:

Kay Come on I know you want it, I know you're up for it, you dirty dirty doctor.

Doctor (*Kylah*) How much did she have to drink?

Fionnula Three tequilas and some gin and tonics but a've a suspicion she'd started a wee bit earlier.

Kay I bet you've had more than a dead man's cock down your trousers, naughty naughty doctor.

Nurse (*Manda*) Will you be quiet – there are people dying here in this ward.

Fionnula Look here, you old boot – you're a nurse not the fucking polis – she was brought here unconscious in an ambulance – so quit terrorising her, ya ugly fat prune.

Nurse (*Manda*) A'm get security.

Fionnula Get the fucking queen, see if we care. We're not going anywhere.

Another bit of 'Don't Bring Me Down' . . .

Chell We'd like to report a theft.

Copper (*Orla*) Is it something you have nicked or were you the victims?

Chell I don't like your attitude, Sergeant. Ah've lost a kilt an' tie to an extreme an' dangerous pervert.

Copper (*Orla*) Would I be correct in supposing you're from the school called Our Lady of Perpetual Succour?

Kylah How do you know that?

Copper (*Orla*) We've just arrested six girls in the fifth year in Jenners with several with food mixers up their jumpers.

Chell Shoplifting. Fucking brilliant, it's no' just us that're in the shite then.

Manda Are you sure you haven't had any uniforms handed in?

Copper (*Orla*) I don't think so.

Chell He's no' exactly gonna come into a polis station with a pile of jizz-stained kilts is he.

More 'Don't Bring Me Down'.

Fionnula I'd like a taxi please at Little France General.

Phone (*Chell*) Name.

Fionnula McConnell.

Phone (*Chell*) Ah have McConnell down here as drunk and disorderly – two females.

Fionnula What do you mean, drunk and disorderly? Yous are a public service, we need to be at the exhibition centre in half an hour. Ma friend had a violent reaction to food.

Phone (*Chell*) Aye. We've just taken a bloke over to Casualty – toe cut off, pishing blood all over an if that's no bad enough, the dirty cunt gets down and does a shite on the taxi floor. An' yur telling me ah cannie choose ma customers.

More 'Don't Bring Me Down'.

Manda Our fucking uniforms've been nicked!

Chell Look, he left a note.

Orla Dirty bastard can't even spell.

Chell Fucking mink run off down the street wi' ma school knickers on his head.

Kylah We can't turn up in skirts as short as these. We'll be fucking arrested.

Chell We'll look more like En Vogue than a convent choir. Where the fuck are Kay and Fionnula?

'Don't Bring Me Down'.

Fionnula Where the fuck's all these buses then?

Kay Do you think it's safe?

Fionnula Anything down from a Barratt house and you think it's Sarajevo.

Kay I think we should turn back, Fionnula.

Druggie (*Kylah*) Hello there, lassies. Can I help you?

Kay Is that a Stone Island logo on your arm?

Druggie (*Kylah*) Aye, exact copy, that's Armani. I'm getting a Versace on the back o' ma neck next week. It's got too expensive to buy the clothes so I just copy the logos for free. Now how can I help yous?

Kay We're very late for a schools choir competition.

Druggie (*Kylah*) What the fuck are yous on, ladies. Listen, if I get caught on the cameras wi' a couple of schoolgirls they'll throw the key away. Let's go into the lobby way.

Fionnula Where you going?

Kay He might be to ring us a taxi.

Fionnula He's a fucking pusher, man.

Kay Wait.

Druggie (*Kylah*) Are you alright?

Fionnula She only had a couple of tequilas – she's not really used to it.

Kay opens her bag and spews into it.

Druggie (*Kylah*) Jesus Christ.

Fionnula What did you do that for?

Kay Ah didn't want to ruin the carpet.

Druggie (*Kylah*) Ruin it? We piss on there rather than risk the fucking lavvies.

Fionnula Yur clothes'll be ruined, Kay.

Kay I need some fresh air.

The Druggie grabs Fionnula.

Druggie (*Kylah*) Excuse me, but I think I'm passionately in love with you or your friend or both of yous, ah don't really have ma emotions about yous sorted out yet. Is there a chance I could ask you out tonight in any combination? I'll give you every drug on me for your phone number.

Fionnula All we need is fifty pence each for the bus fare.

Druggie (*Kylah*) That's what I call a bargain . . . Write it here.

She writes a number.

. . . Chell. That's the most beautiful thing on ma arm. I'm Harry. I'll call you and make a little trip up and see you. You or your friend there, doesn't really matter.

More 'Don't Bring Me Down'.

Fionnula Jesus Christ, Kay. Are you trying to get us killed?

Gurl 1 (*Chell*) What fucking school yous from?

Fionnula Oh no.

Gurl 2 (*Manda*) Look at the state of her –

Kylah Are you oan drugs?

Kay No. I've only had a few gin and tonics.

Gurl 2 (*Manda*) Gin and tonics?!

Fionnula Look. Ah'll square wi yous, sorry for being in yur patch but we got spewin' drunk and had to go to the hospital and we're just trying to get into town cos our teacher's'll murder us.

Gurl 2 (*Chell*) Fuck that. We'll have your money.

Kay Now look here, we have a very important competition to get to.

Fionnula We don't have any money. Just fifty pence for our bus fare.

Gurl 2 (*Chell*) You musta had plenty money for your gin and fucking tonics.

Kay It's in my bag.

Fionnula Oh no.

She hands over the bag. The girl looks in it.

Gurl 1 (*Chell*) For fuck's sake.

Gurl 3 (*Kylah*) You get it.

Gurl 1 (*Manda*) You get it.

Gurl 4 (*Orla*) A'm no' putting my hand in there.

Gurl 2 (*Manda*) Fuck that. We'll just have the bus money.

Fionnula We just got given it off your man, Harry.

Gurl 2 (*Manda*) Harry Reid.

Fionnula Aye, he's in there – ma number's on his arm.

Gurl 2 (*Manda*) Oh fuck. Leave it, Mary.

Aye away you go. A'm giving you this back no' cos I'm shitting it off the man. We're just supporting the arts.

Kay What a fucking arsehole. What a stupid fucking total fucking arsehole.

Fionnula C'mon, Kay. It's not that bad. OK, we'll be in trouble but we'll look back on this . . . with pride.

Kay Fionnula. I'm pregnant.

Fionnula Pregnant?!

Kay About nine weeks. That's where I was today, a place for abortions. I went in but I couldn't do it. I kept thinking of my mam and dad. They're are such fucking Catholics. Dad's in a pro-life doctors' group. Fi, I've totally fucking fucked it.

Fionnula *And she started crying.*

Kay It's a total disaster, my whole life is a total disaster area – in two months it's just gone crazy. Drinking an smoking like this with a wee baby in me.

Fionnula Shush . . .

Kay For all my parents being posh up Pulpit Hill, all the good grades and cello lessons, now I'm just like Shuna MacLaughlin. I may as well've been born on the estate!

Fionnula *And she cried and I looked at her and I thought: I'm gonna fuck her. It's only a matter of time but I'm actually gonna fuck her.*

Kylah One, two, three . . .

'Don't Bring Me Down' finale. They suddenly find themselves at the Conference Centre, facing Sister Codron.

Manda We were in this man's house and he locked himself in the bathroom and we went into see this other man who was standing naked upside down with an enormous erection, Sister, and he fell over and cut off his toe.

Fionnula And apparently shat on a taxi floor.

Kay I wasn't there, Sister. I was in hospital with acute alcoholic poisoning, we couldn't get a taxi cos I'd been sick in my bag.

Orla And when we came out someone stole our uniforms.

Kylah We weren't actually wearing them at the time.

Chell Some bloke was running away with them on his heed.

Manda And this is all we have to wear, Sister.

They burst into Vaughan Williams' 'O Taste and See'.

O taste and see
O taste and see how gracious the Lord is
Blest is the man that trusteth in Him
O taste and see how gracious the Lord is
Blest is the man that trusteth in Him.

Fionnula starts speaking over the top of the rest of the hymn

Fionnula We got disqualified in Round One when Kay threw up during the Vaughan Williams. And Our Ladies got a five-year ban from the competition. In one way we got what we wanted, but as we went back on the bus, Kay sat there pregnant, Manda trying to get over that Kay had slept with her sister, all of us already hungover, it really started to dawn on us: we were in dire fucking trouble.

Kylah We're completely fucked.

Chell They'll stop us seeing each other.

Orla It's a complete disaster.

Kay We're all gonna get expelled.

Manda I still can't believe she shagged my sister.

Fionnula Look, ladies, who gives a fuck if we get expelled? What does it matter anyway? Who the fuck cares what we do? This is our lives and we're young and we're horny as fuck – sod the wanking nuns and sod wer parents, what do they know? We're us, and we're alive here and now. I say stuff it, girls – if we are gonna get expelled, let's make a fucking night of it.

All The Mantrap!

Kay goes through but the Bouncer stops the others.

Bouncer (*Fionnula*) Hang on. ID, ladies.

Fionnula C'mon we were in here two weeks ago.

Bouncer (*Fionnula*) Ah don't recognise you.

Kay Is there a problem?

Fionnula Look, this is daft, a'm eighteen and I come here all the time.

Bouncer (*Fionnula*) You don't look eighteen to me.

Fionnula What's your problem – it's middle of the week, you've let all kinds of psychos in there but you're making a scene for a bunch of girls in a group?!

Bouncer (*Fionnula*) If you're no' eighteen you don't get in, it's the law – a'm only doing ma job. You look eighteen so you're in, but you and you can forget it. And you look about twelve.

Fionnula Just watch it. She had cancer.

Chell She was cured at Lourdes.

Bouncer (*Fionnula*) I don't care if she was cured in the tap room of the Barrels – she's not coming in here. It's full of fucking sailors.

Fionnula Oh come on. We're all the same ages.

Bouncer (*Fionnula*) Yous two can go in.

Fionnula That's fucking ridiculous.

Bouncer (*Fionnula*) Move along inside, ladies.

Manda holds back.

Are you going in or what?

Orla You go, Manda.

Bouncer (*Fionnula*) The rest of yous, off to your mammies.

Fionnula, Manda and Kay go in.

Chell Come on, if we go round the back and all pile up the seaweed we can get in through the bog window.

Come on, pile it up.

Kylah It fucking stinks.

Chell More.

Orla Posh folk eat this, you know.

Chell There's always some over there.

Kylah and Orla go to get more as Chell attends to the pile. She reels back and cries out.

Orla What is it?

Chell I can see my dad!

Orla Which one?

Chell Ma dead daddy. In the seaweed there. There he is!

Kylah Chell. Chell.

Orla Stop, Chell, it's OK.

Chell I swear it was my daddy.

Kylah There's nothing there.

Kylah and Orla calm her down, each of her friends helping her.

Chell A'm sorry. Yous'll think I'm mental.

Kylah It must be all the sea stuff. It must've brought it back to you.

Chell I swear ah saw him right there, buried in it, staring out at me.

Orla It's OK. It was probably a crab or something –

Chell is still breathing deeply, trying to get hold of herself.

Kylah Are you OK, Chell?

Chell A'm alright. C'mon, let's get in there before they start the slow dances.

Kylah *So with a little bit of difficulty –*

Orla *We climbed in through the very small bog window.*

We twist perspective and are inside the club.

Name of fuck. Look at it.

Kylah This is absolutely hopeless.

Chell Where the fuck're all the submareeners?

Fionnula Tucked up in their spunky wee bunks. When he said sailors, he meant those fucking moaners off the herring boats.

Manda What a fucking let-down.

Kay What we gonna do now? We haven't even got money for drinks.

Chell Fuck it, let's dance!

They sing 'Shine a Little Love' by the Electric Light Orchestra. The other girls clear off the floor. Fionnula grabs Kay.

End of 'Shine a Little Love'.

Fionnula Kay.

Come and dance with me.

Kay joins Fionnula on the dance floor.

Kiss me.

They kiss. The dry ice envelops them. Out of the dry ice Orla, Manda, Chell and Kylah emerge.

Chell Fuckin' hell. Have you seen them two?

Manda Shows how desperate it is. Fionnula's having to cop off with Kay frigging Clarke.

Chell What now?

Orla We can't just go home.

Manda The bouncer says he's got some magic mushroom lager. He just lives across the way.

Orla I can't have magic mushroom lager. I've got to meet Chopper. He's coming up on the first train.

Manda Just come for a bit. I really fancy him.

Chell You must be fucking joking, Manda. There's no way any of us are going anywhere near that cunt's house –

Kay and Fionnula walk home.

Fionnula *So I held Kay's hand and we walked up Pulpit Hill.*

It's steep enough.

Kay You should see it in winter. It gets so slippy it takes half an hour to get down. The winter I got the perm, by the time I'd got to the bottom all the mousse in my hair would get frozen. That was the Christmas my ear started to hurt so bad Dad took me to see Dr Drumvargie on

Christmas Eve and he looked right in an' he realised there was something there and he took out this tiny beautiful pearl from right in my ear.

Fionnula Never! How was it there?

Kay Must've been there since I was little. My mum never had pearls so it was a mystery where it came from.

Fionnula That's beautiful.

Kay C'mon. Let's go in.

Bouncer's house – stoned music. Kylah, Chell and Manda are stoned. Orla is sitting like a spare part.

Chell Oh fuck. I'm off my friggin' tits.

Manda Awww!

Bouncer (*Fionnula*) OK, girls – which one of yous is gonna sleep wi' me?

Kylah The problem is we only fuck human beings.

Manda Oh, the fuckin' room's spinning.

Bouncer (*Fionnula*) Look, ladies, if I'm going to let yous in on Saturday ah might just need a wee bit of encouragement.

The Bouncer goes to his room. Manda stands.

Manda I'll do it!

Chell Fuckin' hell, Manda!

Manda Come with me.

She grabs the Bouncer and they go out. Chell and Kylah burst into laughter.

Kylah Fucking state of her.

Chell She's off her fucking tits.

Orla I can't believe she's gone in there.

Kylah Fucking hell – what's this?

Chell Sparklers! Let's light them.

Kay brings them on.

Fucking hell, brilliant.

All Weeeeeee!

A moan from the back room.

Chell Look, there's a whole box of fireworks.

Kay brings on the fireworks.

Orla Oh no!

Chell Let's do a display!

Orla Not in here, Chell!

Kylah *But she lit them anyway.*

Orla *And while Manda lost her virginity to the grot bouncer, we had a display.*

All Hallelulah, hallelulah, hallelulah!

The display, while Manda does a burst of the 'Hallelulah Chorus'.

Chell Shit. The plants are on fucking fire. Jesus fuck. Get on the ground – we'll suffocate.

They get down on to their knees.

Kylah Crawl to the bedroom.

They crawl to the bedroom.

Bouncer (*Fionnula*) Fuckin' hell – more of yous! What's that smoke?

Chell Fireworks, ya daft cunt.

Kylah The whole place is on fire. One of them's gone out the window.

Bouncer (*Fionnula*) Jesus, we'll be busted. All those plants next door are cannabis.

As the smoke clears we are in Kay's bedroom. Kay and Fionnula. Music changes to romantic music.

Kay Mum and Dad aren't back till Friday.

Fionnula Christ, were all those paintings on the stairs there, real?!

Kay Yes, they were Grandpa Mike's. That's where he lived in the Grampians. We used to go to his farm every summer.

Fionnula Wow. Look at the view. You can see the whole Port, the Complex, everything. It must be a good feeling looking down on everything.

Kay Not really. My mum's always complaining I keep the curtains closed.

Fionnula It's like another world up here – all this stuff. This room. With you in it. It's amazing what can change in a day.

Kay (*starts to be unnerved*) I've got some wine up here. Do you want some?

Fionnula (*confesses*) Kay, I think you are a really amazing person. And just being near you, just looking at you is – amazing. You're beautiful, Kay.

Kay Stop, Fionnula. You know I like you. But I don't really think this is right. I don't know if I fancy girls. I think I might have just been a little bit drunk.

Fionnula Really?

Kay A'm sorry, Fionnula.

Fionnula *And ma heart was breaking I didn't know what to say so I said:*

No, it's alright. I better go.

Kay No. Please. I want to play you something.

Fionnula *And she took her cello and she played, and I just stood there, listening.*

We hear the Prelude to Bach's first Cello Suite. The girls accompany with an arrangement of 'Agnus Dei' and Fionnula talks over . . .

And I listened to her play and it was beautiful, sad and beautiful, but I listened and I felt alright, the music was like a gift to me to say: it's alright to be you – it's alright to be who you are. And I cried. And I realised they don't actually teach us anything about love. OK, they tell you about sex and everything, but really with love you're none the wiser, no one really knows what love is, do they? Love is like this big mystery at the centre of the world, huge and silent – there at the centre of everything – like God.

Fionnula hears the girls sing the words of 'Agnus Dei'. She translates them:

Agnus Dei, Lamb of God.
Agnus Dei, Lamb of God, who takes away the sins
    of the world, have mercy upon us.
Agnus Dei, Lamb of God, who takes away the sins
    of the world, have mercy upon us.
Agnus Dei, Lamb of God, who takes away the sins
    of the world, have mercy upon us.
Agnus Dei, Lamb of God, who takes away the sins
    of the world, have mercy upon us.
Agnus Dei, Lamb of God, who takes away the sins
    of the world . . . grant us peace.

The music finishes.

Chell *Four o'clock. In the morning The station.*

Orla You came.

Chopper (*Manda*) Aye.

Orla What's that?

Chopper (*Manda*) That's the budgie.

Orla No, what's that?

Chopper (*Manda*) Me ghetto-blaster. I like to come prepared. So what you been up to?

Orla Well, we got kicked out of the competition and we came back, climbed through the Mantrap window, then two of my best friends turned out to be lezzers, then we went to a bouncer's flat, drank magic mushroom lager and nearly burnt it down.

And my best mate shagged him. And then it's now.

Chopper (*Manda*) So what shall we do?

Orla I thought we could walk up to this old fallen-down castle place.

Chopper OK.

Orla *So he carried the budgie and the ghetto-blaster up the coast.*

Chopper (*Manda*) So this is your famous folly, then?

Orla Is it famous?

Chopper (*Manda*) Oh aye, McCaig's Folly. It's very famous. It was built by this mega-rich guy in 1897 to give work to the stonemasons cos they were all on the dole but it never got finished because he snuffed it from angina pectoris. It has two tiers of lancet arches – forty-four on the top and fifty on the bottom –

73

Orla How do you know that?

Chopper (*Manda*) I'm very interested in ancient history.

Along here's where they reckon Fingal used to tie up his dog.

Orla Fingal?

Chopper (*Manda*) The legendary giant. It's supposed to be haunted by the Green Lady and a Black Hand.

Orla A Black Hand?

Chopper (*Manda*) Aye, a big black hand that chases ya. Don't ya believe in ghosts?

Orla Not really, but just the night Chell saw her dead daddy in a pile of seaweed. I *feel* like a ghost sometimes.

Chopper (*Manda*) Did you know that recent excavations have shown that this castle was refortified in the late thirteenth century . . .

Orla Would you like to screw me?

Chopper (*Manda*) Here?! Are you sure?

Orla Don't you want to?

Chopper (*Manda*) It's a bit damp.

Orla We can use the blanket off the budgie.

Chopper (*Manda*) We can't do that, it might get a chill.

Orla Well, just put your jacket down or something.

Chopper (*Manda*) OK. Hang on.

You know I've never done it before.

Orla Neither have I.

Chopper (*Manda*) Thank God for that. I didn't want to show myself up or anything.

Orla It's alright. I just want to try it once . . .

Chopper (*Manda*) What?

Orla Nothing. Just lie down, will you?

He takes his jacket off and puts it down neatly, lies down, then sits up.

What you doing?

Chopper (*Manda*) Just putting some music on. For the atmosphere.

The girls start singing 'Wild West Hero' by the Electric Light Orchestra.

Orla *And we did it. It didn't seem to last very long. But I liked it. So we just lay there listening to the music . . .*

They continue singing 'Wild West Hero'. In an interlude during the song, we see Kay and Fionnula.

Kay Bye. Are you sure you don't want to stay? You can stay in the spare room.

Fionnula Nah, I promised to meet Orla.

Kay Thanks – for everything.

Fionnula No, thank you. It's weird, isn't it – that sad things can be beautiful and beautiful things can be sad.

Kay Don't be sad. We've got our whole lives ahead of us.

'Wild West Hero' ends.

Orla *The final scene.*

The station buffet. Six o'clock.

Station Guy (*Kay*) Morning.

Orla Morning.

Fionnula So how was it? Did you actually do it?

Orla Aye. It was great and everything but I don't feel very different. I thought doing it, something would happen.

Fionnula What did you think would happen?

Orla That I'd feel more grown up or something.

Fionnula What do you feel?

Orla Sad.

Fionnula, my sickness has come back.

Fionnula Orla?!

How do you know?

Orla I just know. And I'm not having that radiation again.

Fionnula Orla . . .

Orla I know – it's really fucking shit. All this time I thought if I just had this one fucking thing and it doesn't make any fucking difference. I'm still going to fucking die.

The others burst in.

Manda, Chell *and* **Kylah** You won't fuckin' believe what happened . . .

I seriously copped off wi' the bouncer, shagged him and really regretted it, then they burned his room down and we went to the bakery and then we were shitting it about getting expelled so we goes what if we went to see Father Ardlui and we went and knocked on his door and telt him what happened.

Fionnula Yous went to see Father Ardlui at five in the morning?!

Kylah He didn't mind. He just listened and started saying all this stuff you won't believe.

Orla What like?

Kylah Weird stuff about there being a shrine in Bosnia Herzegovina. Like Lourdes and people come. And he started asking us if we ever had dreams like religious dreams and then he asked us straight out –

Fionnula Asks what?

Kylah He says if we lie he'd get us off with Condom and the Superior.

Fionnula Lie about what?

Kylah That we all saw some sort of apparition of the Virgin Mary so he can take it to the church and if they approve it they can build a shrine and get folk coming here all year round, hotels, airports and all that, like in Knock.

Fionnula Where?

Kylah Knock. In Ireland.

Fionnula He asked you to pretend you'd seen a miracle?

Orla What did yous say?

Chell I asked him if we would get a McDonald's. And he said yes!

Fionnula Did you agree?

Chell Nut. We told him to fuck off. We're no angels but we're no lying about a poxy dump like Our Lady's.

Manda Fucking classic.

Station Guy (*Kay*) What can I get yous for breakfast, ladies?

Kylah Just a cup of tea, please. We've spent all our money.

Station Guy (*Kay*) Growing girls like you need a nice bowl of Scottish porridge courtesy of British fucking Rail. No one comes in here till eight anyways. Want some wee beers, I can put them in Coke cups for yous.

All Yes please!

Station Guy (*Kay*) Five beers and five Scottish porridges.

Here's a pound for the jukebox. It looks like it's heavy metal but I've changed everything to reggae classics. I love seeing the bikers' faces when they've just put a quid's worth in.

Fionnula Thanks.

Chell I was saying it's goan' be a cracker today, we should go out Tulloch Ferry to ma sister's place, paddle in the river and that –

We'd get expelled anyway with these clothes on – so fuck it – we could catch the twelve twenty-five out to Kilchoan, it's only a wee walk up the bridle path on a day like this.

Orla Aye, let's go for it. I'll get some money out of the cashpoint and we can get some Hooches.

Kylah Aye, we'll go swimming.

The cheers are rolling.

Manda Fuck Condom and all the rest of them.

As they cheer again the Station Guy shouts, urging them on . . .

Station Guy (*Kay*) Go for it, girls. SMASH THE FUCKING SYSTEM!

Chell Get the records on!

Fionnula steps forward . . .

Fionnula I put a quid in and up came this record we'd all heard before. But somehow it seemed different.

They sing along to the reggae song on the jukebox.

And they sang, none appearing much worse for wear, as the day's sun came silvering over the bay and the tips of the back-country hills already in full summer flush – in this time of their lives.

The End.